IF I SEE LAUNDRY IN THE HAMPER

If I See Laundry in the Hamper

Erin Hicks

CONTENTS

IF I SEE LAUNDRY IN THE HAMPER PART 1

If I see laundry in the hamper, I consider putting it in the washing machine. Then I remember that the weather is getting colder, and I need to go dig out our winter clothes bins so I can wash the winter clothes as well.

If I go to get out the bins, I will need to clean the storage area so I can get to the bins.

And if I am cleaning the storage area, I will need to put the stuff in the den so I can organize it all.

If I put everything in the den, I will need to find a home for some of the things the kids left lying around, so I may as well clean the den.

While I am cleaning the den, I will find the jewelry box I accidentally left in there when I let my daughter borrow my earrings.

When I go to put away the box, I remember that I need to clean out the dressers and put away most of our summer clothes. But it's Georgia so I'm sure I will still need shorts and short sleeved shirts for at least a month.

If I clean out my dresser, I will need to clean OFF my dresser as well because it's a mess and I need to put away the jewelry box.

If I clean off my dresser, I will definitely make a mess on my floor and need to vacuum and sweep.

If I get out the broom and vacuum, I probably need to sweep and vacuum the bedroom and laundry room as well.

If I vacuum the rooms, I will remember I need to mop because it's been a while since I mopped.

If I do sweep and mop my bedroom I must sweep and mop the bathroom because they are attached.

If I sweep and mop my bathroom, I will need to clean the entire bathroom, the cabinets and clean off the counter, the toilet and the tub.

If I clean the tub, I need to remove the jets and scrub them, scrap the caulk off the tub and put new mildew resistant caulk down because its gross and has needed to be fixed for several months.

If I clean the tub I should probably go ahead and change the fixtures because they are very loose and rusted. Then I will need to go to the store and get the fixtures.

If I am going to go to the store, I should make a shopping list.

If I am making a shopping list, I will need to figure out what is for dinner.

While I'm searching the kitchen for what we will eat I notice that the table needs to be cleaned.

As I'm cleaning the table, I go to throw the trash away and realize that I need to take the trash out.

As I'm taking the trash out, I walk past the fish tank, and I remember that I need to feed the fish.

As I am feeding the fish, I notice the water is low and I need to put water in the tank.

As I am putting water in the tank, I realize it needs to be cleaned.

As I begin to clean the tank, I get fish slime on my shirt and I go to change.

But first I will need to shower and then put on clean clothes, which I don't have because the dirty clothes are still in the hamper.

So, instead I'll do a puzzle.

DEVOTIONS

As a homeschool mom, with ADHD I tend to go through this process a lot, as in daily. As funny as it seems when I talk about the challenges (and it truly is funny), the flight, fight, or freeze response is very real and very frustrating. To have a million thoughts racing through your mind and just freeze (or get angry or run away and hide) and be unable to do any of them is truly more than frustrating. And even though I have yet to figure out a good consistent solution for the problem, I have found that if I make a list of all the things, I have done that day I do feel more accomplished. No matter how small the task is, getting out of bed, getting shoes on, drinking water, making a list...I can check off a lot of things that I accomplished and that makes me more motivated to do the next thing. It may not be the next "most important" thing like laundry, but I will do something. So, be encouraged. You are not alone. And you are amazing just the way you are. Here are some encouraging notes for the next 15 days.

DAY 1– YOU ARE CHOSEN!

Isaiah 41:9... I have called to you and said, "you are my servant. And I have chosen you, not thrown you away!"

He has chosen you and not thrown you away. It's kind of awesome to know that he will never see you as trash but chosen. Chosen by the Creator of heaven and earth, chosen by the King of Kings, chosen by Lord of Lords. You were never a mistake, and not a happenstance. If you are chosen, you can't be trash. Trash is useless, it is waste that is broken and un-needed. You are not waste; you are never unneeded. You are wanted. When you go to the grocery store you purchase what you need and what you want, not things you want to throw away. (Unless it's bananas, we all throw out bananas). You are not trash, don't act like it. So, now go do the ONE thing you choose. Whatever that may be, eat, shower, do laundry, play a game because you can.

DAY 2- YOU ARE NOT ALONE!

Isaiah 41:10 ...So do not be afraid. I am here, with you; don't be dismayed, for I am your God. I will strengthen you, help you. I am here with my right hand to hold you up.

You are not alone, ever. You may feel alone, you may feel like you are doing everything by your-self, or even feel like no one understands what you are experiencing. However, He says that He is here with you and that He strengthens you and holds you up. So, when you feel weak or tired or like you can't go on, he is strengthening you AND (here is the coolest part) He is holding you up with his right hand...and WHO is at the right hand of the Father? That's right, the SON. Jesus is who is holding you up. He is there to lean on, to support the weight so you can do what you need to do. He understands and walks with us and helps us so we are never left to do it alone. Enjoy his company as he walks with you, enjoy his presence and his help. Do something and feel accomplished because he's helping you through today.

DAY 3– YOU ARE BEING MADE INTO SOMETHING POWERFUL AND INCREDIBLE!

Isaiah 41:14-16 ...you have nothing to fear. Eternal One: I will help you. I am One who saves you, the Holy One of Israel. I will turn you into a formidable threshing sledge with brand new sharp blades that will mow down entire mountains and turn the hills into chaff. You will separate value from waste, and a great wind and a strong storm will take away what is useless and unimportant.

He is working on you. He's turning you into something powerful and strong. He's refining you. If you allow him to take away all the useless and unimportant things, you will see your value. He is making a way for YOU to separate the value from the waste. Look for your value when you are irritated about the things you can't do or don't feel like you can do. Don't look at the negative, look at your value! Be incredible today!

DAY 4- YOU HAVE JOY WHEN YOU TAKE PRIDE IN HIM!

Isaiah 41:16 ...You will take joy in the Eternal. You will glow with pride in the Holy One of Israel.

Sometimes it is hard for us to aim our confidence in the right direction. We feel like our self-confidence is important and we try so hard to do things right and do them well so that others will appreciate us in order to build up that self-confidence. When it's really GOD-confidence that we need. God-confidence is not dependent on how well we do, or how others respond to us. God-confidence is only dependent on who God is. If we allow ourselves to take pride in who He is and what He does, then we will walk around full of joy. Knowing and trusting in the fact that He is perfect, and he always does what He says is what gives us the feeling of pride in Him. Take pride in the fact that He is your Maker, Promise Keeper, Light in the darkness, your Friend, and your Father. Make today awesome and choose joy!

DAY 5- YOU ARE UNIQUELY CREATED!

Psalm 139:13-14 You knitted me together in my mother's womb long before I took my first breath. I will offer You my grateful heart, for I am Your unique creation, filled with wonder and awe. You have approached even the smallest details with excellence; Your works are wonderful; I carry this knowledge deep within my soul. You see all things; nothing about me was hidden from You.

Ephesians 2:10 For we are the product of His hand, heaven's poetry etched on lives, created in the Anointed, Jesus, to accomplish the good works God arranged long ago.

God created you in such a unique and beautiful way. You are not like any other person on this planet that ever has been or ever will be. You are made to be different. Embrace your individuality. Look in the mirror and tell yourself that you are an amazingly uniquely created mom, woman, wife, etc. You are not just created, but you are KNOWN, everything about you, down to the smallest detail, even the number of eye lash hairs and how they sit on your eyelids. Carry this knowledge deep within your soul, that you are crafted by the Savior and fully known.

DAY 6- YOU ARE AMAZINGLY CREATIVE!

Genesis 1:26 Now let Us conceive a new creation-humanity- made in Our image, fashioned according to Our likeness. And let Us grant them authority over all the earth-

God says we are created in Their image. The image of the Father, Son, and Holy Spirit. One of His characteristics is creativity. He creatively made every single flower, animal, cloud in the sky, etc. Every single vein in a leaf and snowflake that falls from the winter sky. You are made to create. So, when you make a meal, read a story, make up a song, arrange furniture, you are being creative. When you start a new hobby, paint a picture, create a schedule or plan your day you are being creative, and you are doing it well! Creativity is not just arts and crafts, its anything you make or create. Don't think, "well, I can't even draw a straight line" or " I can't even make dinner." These negative thoughts are not what God is saying about you. He says that He created you to BE creative so, go do something creative!

DAY 7- YOU ARE DEEPLY LOVED AND TREASURED!

Zephaniah 3:17 The Eternal your God is standing right here among you, and He is the champion who will rescue you. He will joyfully celebrate over you; He will rest in His love for you; He will joyfully sing because of you like a new husband.

1 John 4:16 We have experienced and we have entrusted our lives to the love of God in us. God is love. Anyone who lives faithfully in love also lives faithfully in God, and God lives in him.

No matter what you have done today, yesterday, ten years ago, 6 months ago, God is still God. He still loves you and treasures you. His love is unending and never failing. He is singing over you joyfully. Don't allow your mind to sink into the thoughts that you are unloved. It is far too easy to listen to our feelings and not listen to truth. Remind your heart that you aren't loved because you did something lovable, you are loved because that is WHO HE IS! God is love and he loves you perfectly. To know that he is singing over you, what a beautiful thing to focus on. What does it sound like to hear God singing over you? What words is he using when he sings? "I love you; you are my treasure, you are the most beautiful, you are creating amazing things, you are so wise and loving, what you do and the work you put in is beautiful to watch." I think these are a few of the things he sings over you. Go share that love with someone else.

DAY 8- YOU ARE HEARING HIS VOICE!

John 10:27 My sheep respond as they hear My voice; I know them intimately, and they follow Me.

John 8: 47 ...If you belong to God's family, then why can't you hear God speak? The answer is clear; you are not in God's family. ...

You may be questioning your life choices. Questioning if you are doing the right thing or the wrong thing. Who am I, what am I supposed to do, did I mess up? Here's the thing, you are hearing his voice. If you are in God's family, then you are hearing his voice. Trust that. What is God saying to you? Did God say to love your family? Yes. Did God say to spend time with Him? Yes. Does God tell you to sin? No. Did God say to eat a ton of junk food? No. We make choices all the time and they have nothing to do with what God is actually saying to us. You may question your choices but remembering that you DO hear Him is so important. Do you think God is telling you to sing a song? Sing it! So, what if you are at home with only your kids, maybe your kids will hear you sing and realize that they want to sing too. Next thing you know everyone is dancing and singing with joy. All because you listened. Read the word, spend time in the quiet. Then trust that you are hearing what he says because you are learning to recognize his voice every single time you read anything in the Word. Do something you think God wants you to do. Start with the basics, show love and kindness.

DAY 9- YOU HAVE EVERYTHING YOU NEED!

Luke 12:31 Since you don't need to worry- about security and safety, about food and clothing- then pursue God's kingdom first and foremost, and these other things will come to you as well.

Philippians 4:19 Know this: my God will also fill every need you have according to His glorious riches in Jesus the Anointed, our Liberating King.

Psalm 34:10 Young lions may grow tired and hungry, but those intent on knowing the Eternal God will have everything they need.

The word says that God has given you everything you need. He provides for you. You don't need to worry where your next meal comes from because He will cover you. Don't worry if your kids will have clothes, He's got you. Trust him! Lean on him. Let him provide for you. He desires to give you the very best. Seek Him and His kingdom first. Know Him. If you know Him, you will Trust Him. Show your family that you trust Him by giving that worry over to God and letting your mind rest.

DAY 10- YOU HAVE DONE WELL! PROGRESS NOT PERFECTION.

2 Peter 3:18 Instead, grow in grace and in the true knowledge of our Lord and Savior Jesus, the Anointed, to whom be the glory, now and until the coming of the new age. Amen

Matthew 5:48 But you are called to something higher; "Be perfect, as your Father in heaven is perfect."

James 3:2 We all stumble along the way. If a person never speaks hurtful words or shouts in anger or profanity, then he has achieved perfection.

We are not perfect. We are to make progress. 2 Peter doesn't say have grace and knowledge, it says GROW. Growing is a slow progression. Yes, we are called to "be perfect" but that is about love and progress. Have you achieved perfection yet? No? Stop looking at every mistake and look at every success. You need to see the progress you have made. Look at where you are now and where you were 5 years ago. Don't see change? That's ok! Sometimes we have a wilderness season. Look at today and choose growth. Find one small thing to change and go for it. Drink water every day, make an effort to read the word daily. One small change makes progress.

DAY 11- YOU CAN'T DO IT ALL, BUT HE CAN!

Proverbs 3:5-6: Place your trust in the Eternal; rely on Him completely; never depend upon your own ideas and inventions. Give Him the credit for everything you accomplish, and He will smooth out and straighten the road that lies ahead.

Romans 8:31-32 So what should we say about all of this? If God is on our side, then tell me: whom should we fear? If He did not spare His own Son, but handed Him over on our account, then don't you think that He will graciously give us all things with Him?

Ezekiel 36:9 I, of course, care about you and will turn My attention on you.

You can't do it all. You cannot be everything for everyone. Cook, house cleaner, teacher, driver, councilor, doctor, personal shopper, financial consultant, administrative assistant, boss, etc. You may think you are supposed to do it all, but you are not. What does it mean to say He is for you? It means you have Him by your side to carry you along. It means he won't just hold your hand while you work but he will guide you and take over the rest. And sometimes that means there's a lot of things that we need to let go of. Listen, Love, and Let it go. THAT is what we are called to do. Listen to Him, Love Him- you-others, Let go of all the junk that you don't need to worry about. Depend on Him, give Him all the credit, He wants to do this for you! Leave room in your heart and mind for peace today as you lay it all down.

DAY 12- YOU CAN REST!

Genesis 2:2 On the seventh day- with the canvas of the cosmos completed- God paused from His labor and rested.

Exodus 33:14 Eternal One: My presence will travel with you , and I will give you rest.

Matthew 11:28 Come to Me, all who are weary and burdened, and I will give you rest.

Are you tired? YOU CAN REST! Don't think that you are not allowed to take a break. Sometimes we are tired because we worked hard, other times it's hormones, occasionally it is stress, or maybe we have spent a lot of brain energy. God rested on the 7th day. And HE is God. How much more do we need rest! We are HUMANS. He said in His presence we can rest. He says He is always with us, so His presence is always here. Take a moment to rest in His presence.

DAY 13- YOU ARE WISE WHEN YOU ASK FOR WISDOM!

Proverbs 1:7 Let us begin. The worship of the Eternal One, the one true God, is the first step toward knowledge. Fools, however, do not fear God and cannot stand wisdom or guidance.

James 1:5 If you don't have all the wisdom needed for this journey, then all you have to do is ask God for it; and God will grant all that you need. He gives lavishly and never scolds you for asking.

Proverbs 2:6 The Eternal is ready to share His wisdom with us, for His words bring true knowledge and insight...

Proverbs 19:8 Whoever gains a wise heart loves his own soul, and whoever preserves understanding experiences true goodness.

You have so much wisdom! And what you don't already have you can access, by asking the Father. The choices you make, the things you do for your family. Your job, your kids, etc. You are wise and can do so much because that is how you were made. Accept the FACT that you are wise. Allow yourself to really believe that you are a wise mother, a wise wife, a wise child of God. Mistakes and poor judgement happen, those don't determine whether you are wise or not. Lay down all those poor choices and mistakes and ask the One who knows ALL things to provide you with what you need to move forward. He is here with all the wisdom and knowledge you need.

DAY 14- IT IS GREAT THAT YOU ARE DOING THINGS DIFFERENTLY THAN THE REST!

Isaiah 43:18 Eternal One: don't revel only in the past or spend all your time recounting the victories of days gone by. Watch closely; I am preparing something new; it's happening now, even as I speak.

Romans 12:2 Do not allow this world to mold you in its own image. Instead, be transformed from the inside out by renewing your mind. As a result, you will be able to discern what God wills and whatever God finds good, pleasing, and complete.

Galatians 6:4 examine your own works so that if you are proud, it will be because of your own accomplishments and not someone else's.

Being unique is great, but doing unique things is even better! We are all gifted in different ways and given different abilities. So, your neighbor has a clean house and cooks dinner every night for her family. You played with Legos and the kids had cereal. You read a book today? Good for you, teaching your family what it means to take care of yourself. You made dinner, awesome! You ordered pizza, amazing! Don't feel like you have to do what they do or "keep up with the joneses." You were not made to do all the same things. Don't compare yourself to them, compare yourself to what God asks of YOU. If you look at what they do, realize that God could be telling them to do different things. And that is awesome! Be different and do different.

DAY 15— YOU ARE ENOUGH!

Job 33:4 ... God's Spirit has fashioned me and the breath of the Highest One imparts life to me.

Romans 8:1 Therefore, now no condemnation awaits those who are living in Jesus the Anointed, the Liberating King, because when you live in the Anointed One, Jesus, a new law takes effect. The law of the Spirit of life breathes into you and liberates you from the law of sin and death.

Romans 8: 38-39 For I have every confidence that nothing- not death, life, heavenly messengers, dark spirits, the present, the future, spiritual powers, height, depth, nor any created thing-can come between us and the love of God revealed in the Anointed, Jesus our Lord.

Esther 4:14 "... Perhaps you have been made queen for such a time as this."

You are enough. It's easy to feel like we are letting others down or not doing enough. It's easy to feel frustrated and sad and lacking. But God created you for such a moment as this. He put YOU in this family, gave YOU that husband and kids, set YOU in that church, made YOU have those friends. You are enough because God made you for this. No guilt, no shame, no condemnation, can separate you from Him. No height, no depth, no created thing can separate you from His Love. He has breathed His life into you. You are full of His life, His breath, His Spirit. You are what He has meant for you to be. Know your worth!

WRAP UP

So, to wrap this up, remember...

You are chosen, never alone, being made into something powerful and incredible, have joy, uniquely created, amazingly creative, deeply loved and treasured, hearing His voice, have everything you need, are making progress, He can do it all through you-He's for you, you can rest, you are wise, you are doing different things and that is awesome, you are enough.

IF I SEE LAUNDRY IN THE HAMPER PART 2

If I see laundry in the hamper, I remember that it is getting colder and want to snuggle in a blanket with my husband and kids.

If I snuggle with my family, I think of a movie we may want to watch.

If I think of a movie we may want to watch, I might make some popcorn.

When I make popcorn, I grab some candy from my secret stash.

When I grab the candy, I notice the dust on the fridge, and I get a glass of water.

When I get the glass of water, I notice that the dishwasher is full, and I don't empty it.

Instead of emptying the dishwasher I go back to snuggle the kids.

I snuggle with the kids, eat the candy (don't share the candy), watch the movie and decide the movie is boring so I read a book.

As I read the book, I realize I may need to shower. It's 3pm and I will take a shower.

After I shower, I may decide I don't want to cook dinner, so I get nothing out of the freezer.

I may sit in my office and type a little. And while I type I notice the time is 6pm and everyone is hungry.

Since everyone is hungry, I tell them to eat cereal or find food.

As we all get our food, I notice the kids have went into their rooms to eat and watch tv.

As they watch tv in their rooms I start to feel guilty for all the things I didn't do.

As I start to feel the guilt, I remember who I am in Christ. I remember that today is only one day. I remember that I am different, unique, and loved.

As I remember all the amazing things about God and His love for me, I hear the still small voice of God telling me that my children and husband are loved and know it, that I am doing good, and that I am making progress.

As I hear these and remember these things, I go hug my kids.

After I hug my kids, I go do a puzzle, because I like to do puzzles. And guess what? There is still laundry in the hamper.

Acknowledgements

Thanks so much to my husband Jeremy for helping me stay committed to finishing things...Primarily this small book.
Thanks to my 3 children Paige, Teagan, and Toby for being my constant inspiration and daily distraction.
Thank you to Jennifer Roach for your encouragement, friendship, and requesting I write my thoughts down and make it a book.
Thank you to Melissa Shultz for letting me text you 4k+ times about random things and still telling me that this book seemed like a good idea.